The Waiting

Room

How much longer will I be here?

Shondra Echols

My Thanks

Thank you for purchasing my very first book!
It is my prayer that everyone who reads this book will be encouraged to stay, pray, press and praise in your Waiting Room!

Special thanks to my husband Ryan for your love and support and your commitment to God and me! Thanks for holding my hand and waiting patiently with me. Your greater is coming! I love you!

Thanks to my sons who taught me how to love patiently and unconditionally. The hand of the Lord is upon each of you; continue to worship Him while you wait!
Breakthrough is coming!
I love you all!

Thanks to my mother for always supporting, loving and praying for me. You are an awesome example of being not weary in well doing, for you have truly reaped because you fainted not! I love you!

Chapter 1

30+ Years of Waiting

I have waited for something or someone my entire life. As a young child I remember anxiously waiting for Christmas and birthdays. I waited and sometimes dreaded the first day of each school year. As a teenager, I waited to use the phone and I waited for friends to call. I've waited to be picked up and I've waited while picking others up. I've waited on buses and trains and worst of all, in major traffic jams.

Waiting! Waiting! Waiting!

You'd think with all the waiting I've done I'd have a great level of patience, but unfortunately I don't.

I have NEVER liked to wait. Do you remember asking your Mom or Dad for something you really wanted? What was their answer? "Just wait until Christmas" or "You'll have to wait until I get paid" or they might even say, "I'll have to wait and see your report card before I say yes".

Why is waiting so hard to do??!!

I am still today asking that question. I have heard that waiting on God builds your faith. I've also heard that you should worship while you wait. But what if you've been waiting for 30 or more years?

After 30 years, your faith should be as high as the Empire State Building and as deep and wide as the Pacific Ocean. After 30 years, you should have Bachelor's, Master's and Doctorate degrees in worship.

What I'm trying to say is 30 years is an EXTREMELY LONG TIME TO WAIT ON ANYTHING!!!

If it hasn't happened in 30 years, chances are it won't happen!

Right?!

Maybe you need to face the facts!

I'm reminded of lyrics from a song by an awesome vocalist and one of my many favorites, Mikki Howard. "…You deserve something better, I kept telling myself. Just be patient true love you'll find…"

But if it's been 30 years, maybe I'm unlovable or I've gotten too old.

Let's explore a few definitions. Now please know that I will keep this book interesting and hopefully humorous. We all could use more laughter in our lives. I will not over burden you with big words and definitions. However, I do think definitions are important so that we are on the same page and you properly understand and receive the message in this book.

According to the Merriam-Webster Dictionary, the definition of **patient** *is manifesting forbearance under provocation or strain. Not hasty or impetuous.* (I like this one.) *Steadfast despite opposition, difficulty, or adversity. Able or willing to bear.*

The Waiting Room

Wait: *to stay in place in expectation of. To serve as waiter for. To remain stationary in readiness or expectation. To pause for another to catch up. To hold back expectantly*

Room: *an extent of space occupied by or sufficient or available for something. A partitioned part of the inside of a building; especially: such a part used as lodging. A suitable or fit occasion or opportunity: chance.*

Revelation Check: So in my waiting room I am serving and remaining in readiness and expectation for my chance! Wow!!!

Now back to the 30 years of waiting. LOL (laughing out loud)!

You may have only been waiting for 1 year or 10 years or 50 years. The point is everyone has their own waiting room. When I think of a waiting room I immediately envision a hospital with a waiting room full of people waiting to see a doctor or waiting to find out the status of their loved ones who are in surgery.

The Waiting Room

The waiting room is usually a dull, small, stressful place where joy is often not found.

In the waiting room, you are more aware of time and often wonder, "What's taking so long?"

Can you imagine being in a hospital waiting room for 30 years?

Surely not!

WHO WOULD WAIT THAT LONG?

Chapter 2

Patience is a Virtue

I remember as a child being told that "patience is a virtue". I never really knew what it meant because I didn't know what a virtue was. Just in case you're saying, "I still don't know what it means", LOL, here's the definition.

Virtue: *a beneficial quality or power of a thing. A commendable quality or trait: merit. Chastity especially in a woman.*

Patience is a beneficial quality, a commendable trait. It's a very commendable thing to be able to sit calmly in a waiting room for hours without complaint when you are in pain needing to see a doctor.

But some of us just cannot do it. We are impatient! We cannot sit still, we have to move around and keep up with the pace of life.

My lifelong dream has been to become a world famous gospel singer. God gave me a beautiful voice!

I know that I can sing. Hundreds of people have agreed and have complimented me on my singing. However, I have yet to record my own music. Why has my dream not been fulfilled?

Every attempt I've made to record my music has come to naught, nothing, nada, no deal! I won't begin to tell you about all the days and nights I've prayed and cried and cried and cried some more! LOL

With each passing year and still no CD my hopes faded little by little. Every new year I would make a resolution about my project, sow a seed and make a declaration that "This will be the year! No more delay!" However, that year and the following years passed and no CD, not even a single.

Sad isn't it?

Now I'm depressed because thousands of dollars have been basically given away to "producers" and I have nothing to show for it.

I began to question God saying, *I'm a TITHER!*

I am born-again, I pray, I live by faith, I make confessions,

I go to church!

God, does this mean I should give up on recording my CD?

What about all the prophecies I've received over the years?

You said I would sing before thousands of people.

You said my music would minister healing.

You said all of this in my twenties.

I am peeking in the window looking at 40!

SHE'S COMING SOON!

WHAT'S GOING ON?!

I'M ABOUT TO BE TOO OLD!!! Or at least I feel like it.

After questioning God and going through this tantrum,

guess what I hear?!

"PATIENCE IS A VIRTUE!"

For real God?! LOL! Our God has a wonderful sense of

humor. ☺

I also hear, *"But let patience have her perfect work, that ye may be perfect and entire, wanting nothing. (James 1:4, KJV)*

Here are some scriptures for meditation:

But let endurance and steadfastness and patience have full play and do a thorough work, so that you may be (people) perfectly and fully developed (with no defects), lacking in nothing. (James 1:4, AMP)

But if we hope for what is still unseen by us, we wait for it with patience and composure. (Romans 8:25, AMP)

For you have need of steadfast patience and endurance, so that you may perform and fully accomplish the will of God, and thus receive and carry away (and enjoy to the full) what is promised. (Hebrews 10:36, AMP)

Chapter 3

The Best Waiter

I love to go out to eat with my family. When my children were younger they would get very excited about going out to eat. They would continually ask me "What time are we going to the restaurant?" "As soon as you are finished cleaning your room and get dressed", was my usual response. Once we get to the restaurant the excitement dies a bit because we have to wait. Sometimes the wait is only a few minutes but sometimes it's an hour or more. Nobody likes to wait especially when you're hungry and ready to eat. After my youngest has played a few games on my cell phone and made a few trips to the lobster tank he's really ready to eat. Finally, our name is called and our table is ready (after waiting 40 minutes). But that wasn't the biggest problem. The hostess seats us and we begin to play the waiting game again. Where is our waitress? After she finally arrives, she doesn't appear to be the friendliest, most

13

cordial person. She is polite but nothing extra. Throughout the meal we have to look for her and ask other servers to "please ask our waitress to come". I'm sure many of you have experienced this scenario or something similar.

What if you were the waiter? What if God were the person waiting on you to serve and wait on Him?

Do you think He'd be please with your service? Or would He have to ask, *"Where is she? She knows I'm here waiting! What's taking her so long to come to Me?" "Does he no longer want to serve Me? I was ready to give him a great tip, but he's not doing a great job of waiting."*

Now you may be thinking, "God wouldn't be in a restaurant." Well I choose to disagree. Our loving Father will go to great lengths to try to get our attention and help us. Back to the scenario. ☺

The whole point of the scenario is to help you see that you are God's waiter. A waiter, by definition, is one that waits on another. As I stated previously, nobody likes to wait, we want what we want NOW!

During my years of waiting I've learned so much about myself. I am a really funny, silly person. I have developed an enormous sense of humor (when it comes to certain things). I'm a writer! I'm a great songwriter, poet and author. I am passionate about prayer. When I pray, I go in! But there are also times when I pray and there's mostly silence. I have learned that I honestly cannot live without God. I know that He loves me and has preserved me for His purposes. I've learned that it's good being me! I am beautiful just the way God made me! Now I still want to lose a few pounds and inches here and there but God made a beautiful woman when He designed me!

I have learned that something in me attracts people. Since God loves people and most people like me then maybe God wants to use me to help people in some way. Maybe it will be through this book. Hopefully you will begin to see that your waiting is not in vain. Right now you are a waiter so decide that you will be the best, most excellent waiter God has. Wait with joy and a smile on your face! Utilize your acting skills, fake it until you make it. Wait without complaint. Don't focus on how long you've been waiting. Remember that God's time is not your time. Wait with purpose!

Meditate on these verses during your wait:

*What I do, God, is wait for You, wait for my Lord, my God-
You will answer! (Psalm 38:9-16, MSG)*

*I wait in hope for your salvation, God.
(Genesis 49:18, MSG)*

*I waited and waited and waited for God. At last He looked;
finally He listened. He lifted me out of the ditch, pulled me
from deep mud. He stood me up on a solid rock to make
sure I wouldn't slip. He taught me how to sing the latest
God-song, a praise-song to our God. More and more
people are seeing this: they enter the mystery, abandoning
themselves to God. (Psalm 40:1-3, MSG)*

*God, the one and only- I'll wait as long as He says.
Everything I need comes from Him, so why not?
He's solid rock under my feet, breathing room for my soul,
an impregnable castle: I'm set for life.
(Psalm 62:1-2, MSG)*

Chapter 4

Why? What's the Purpose?

So what's really going on? What's the purpose for this wait? The God we serve is almighty, omnipotent, and powerful; the creator of all that is, was and will be. He is the ONLY true and living God! Since God is "all that" why doesn't He just give me what I'm asking for? Why do we have to pray and wait for God to answer? Why do people get sick with serious diseases and have to go through painful treatments in search of healing? Some go through years of chemotherapy or years of dialysis, waiting on a new kidney.

Our God is God, what is the purpose of this painful wait? Why do the righteous seem to be the ones most afflicted? I don't understand the purpose or reason for this sickness. If there's a lesson for me to learn, can I learn it without going through this pain? Is this pain presently in my life for a purpose? This word PURPOSE keeps coming up. I often hear people say, "You were born for a purpose" or "Find your purpose", and "Live on purpose". What is purpose? Purpose is defined as "the reason for which something exists or is done, made, used, etc.; an intended or desired result; end; aim; goal." Synonyms of the word purpose are: ambition, aspiration, big idea, design, desire, destination, determination, direction, dream, expectation, function, goal, hope, intent, mission, objective, plan, scope and target.

So with this new found information I can ask God, "What is the destination (purpose), direction, mission and expectation of this pain? When you're in the waiting room of pain you honestly just want to get out of it! You are desperate for a miracle or a breakthrough to come. In the end you know you will receive your healing but your route to healing requires waiting. While waiting you must discover the purpose; the destination, direction, mission and the expectation that the Father has for you. What do you mean?

Thanks for asking! While waiting, praying and serving God, the more you commune with Him and His word you will discover your purpose. You'll discover the destination- where you're going; the direction- exactly what He wants you to do; the mission- strategies, how to do it, why you have to go this route; and the expectation- what God is looking for and expecting from you.

So in this chapter I have asked a lot of questions. I could spend hours, days, or months asking why. But Ecclesiastes chapter 3 provides the best answer to our "why".

v.1: Everything that happens in this world happens at the time God chooses.

v.2: He sets the time for birth and the time for death,

v.3: the time for killing and the time for healing...

v.11: He has set the right time for EVERYTHING. He has given us a desire to know the future, but never gives us the satisfaction of fully understanding what He does.

v. 12: So I realized that all we can do is to be happy and do the best we can while we are still alive. (Ecclesiastes 3:1-3, 11-12 GNB)

Here are more scriptures for meditation.

May He give you what your heart desires and fulfill your

whole purpose. (Psalm 20:4, HCSB)

I call to God Most High, to God who fulfills (His purpose)

for me. (Psalm 57:2, HCSB)

The Lord has prepared everything for His purpose- even
the wicked for the day of disaster.
(Proverbs 16:4, HCSB)

The Lord of Hosts has sworn: As I have purposed; so it will
be; as I have planned it, so it will happen. (Isaiah 14:24,
HCSB)

Chapter 5

Hold On, Help is On the Way!

I remember over 13 years ago when my husband and I married. We were in love, excited, optimistic and ready to begin our new life together. We didn't expect nor anticipate all the trials and issues we would face throughout the years. Some of the challenges I faced were at times so painful and overwhelming that I considered leaving my love and giving up on all we said would be. Every time I cried and prayed to God, He would say "Wait", "I got you", "Hold on, don't give up", "Help is on the way". It was those little reassurances and prayer that sustained my family.

When believers unite in marriage the enemy instantly goes into attack mode seeking an entrance to establish his plans. When you know and truly believe your marriage is ordained by God you must stand your ground against every attack of the devil with the word of God. Yep, this is easier said than done because you may be "seeing" different than what God has said!

This is the crucial time that you must decide to live by vision and not by sight.

What is the vision that God has given you for your marriage, family, your healing, ministry, or your career? Write it down, print it out and post it throughout your home or office.

This is what you must focus on while waiting for everything and everyone to line up to God's perfect will! VISION!

If you live by sight, what you see will eventually kill you! I remember being so stressed out at times to the point of seeing a psychiatrist. I've been on muscle relaxers, anti-depressants, pain killers and antacids.

I didn't want to wait on God! I wanted to fix things myself. I wanted to please everyone and wanted to be happy. I didn't want to wait and didn't always do what God was instructing me to do.

Then one day (years after I almost killed myself with stress and worry) I got the revelation that I have the power to create my own happiness. I have the authority and anointing to speak to situations and they MUST CHANGE! I got the revelation that stressing hasn't profited me anything but gray hair and fine lines! (Lol) As soon as I truly began to operate in my new found freedom, HELP CAME! Stressful situations and people were moved! Doors of opportunity began to open for me! I now realize that the waiting room is a place of preparation, a place of peace and a place of growth!

I no longer depend on my husband, children or friends to make me happy or give me joy.

My joy is rooted and grounded in God's promises for my life!

My joy comes from knowing!

I know that God loves ME!

I know God has MY back!

I know that Jesus is daily making intercession for ME!

I know that it is God's will for ME to be healed and prosperous!

I know that I am the seed of Abraham and therefore an heir to the promises God made to Abraham and his seed!

I know that I can cast all my cares on the Lord for He cares for ME!

I know that God has a great plan and purpose for MY life!

I know that I don't have to be sick, stressed, depressed, worried, angry, defeated, depleted, heated, mistreated, and cheated!

These are just a few of the things that I "know" that cause me to have JOY! I will hold on, because help is on the way!

Here are a few scriptures for meditation.

I lift my eyes toward the mountains, Where will my help come from? My help comes from the Lord, the Maker of heaven and earth. (Psalm 121:1-2, HCSB)

For we live by believing and not by seeing. (II Corinthians 5:7, NLT)

Faith is the confidence that what we hope for will actually happen; it gives us assurance about things we cannot see. (Hebrews 11:1, NLT)

Therefore, since we are surrounded by such a huge crowd of witnesses to the life of faith, let us strip off every weight that slows us down, especially the sin that so easily trips us up. (Hebrews 12:1, NLT)

Take (with me) your share of the hardships and suffering (which you are called to endure) as a good (first-class) soldier of Jesus Christ. (II Timothy 2:3, AMP)

This vision is for a future time. It describes the end, and it will be fulfilled. If it seems slow in coming, wait patiently, for it will surely take place. It will not be delayed. (Habakkuk 2:3, NLT)

Chapter 6

Re-decorating the Room

Most women and some men love to decorate. But honestly it's never really been my thing. Don't get me wrong, I love to see beautifully decorated homes and buildings. However, the gift to put it all together perfectly wasn't given to me. But lately I've begun learning how to beautify places and areas in my life that have been destroyed and decayed in the storms of life. When you're waiting on something (anything) good to happen in your life, the desire or excitement for it begins to diminish over time. I remember a time in my life when I did the bare minimum to adorn and beautify myself. I have never let myself go, in the sense of looking bad but I just didn't desire to do the extra: make-up, lingerie, hair appointments, etc. Why do it? What will it profit me? Nothing good comes my way! I'm still waiting on God to do this one thing for me and after all these years it hasn't happened so to heck with everything else!

I don't care anymore because God and nobody else care about me! For years I lived in my own private pity party. Nothing was beautiful about my life. Then about a year or two ago I decided that change had to begin in me. I stopped feeling sorry for myself and began the process of reprogramming my mind from depression to joy and happiness! I even had to limit or even stop having phone conversations with people that always had an issue or problem to place on my shoulders. I learned to encourage them, change the subject or end the conversation. Now that may seem a bit harsh but you have to realize that I too have my own issues, weights, hurts and battles that I was currently evicting from my mind and life. I could not afford to take on any more stress especially if the person wasn't ready or willing to heed godly advice and release it to the Lord.

The Waiting Room

When you are re-programming your mind you must be intentional and deliberate in the things you do, say, see and hear. Remember the enemy is always looking for an opening. Give him no opportunity or entry into your life. Let's go back to re-decorating the room. Now that my mindset has changed regarding my circumstances, my surroundings must also change. During Spring Break 2014, I painted some areas in the first floor of my house! It was long overdue and I was tired of looking at scratches and scuff marks on my walls. In another week or two I will begin painting areas on the second floor. You may be wondering why I'm sharing this and what's the significance? I am so glad you asked! We are currently in our personal waiting room, right? So since you have decided to wait on God and not give up, cave in or quit, re-decorate your waiting room.

Pull depression and sadness off the walls!

Rip up resentment and torment from the floors!

Spray away death with the fragrance called abundant life!

Replace the window shades with sheers so that the sun

(Son) can shine through!

The sun is your reminder that MORNING ALWAYS

COMES!

Let the Son shine in!

Re-decorating your waiting room can be a physical

transformation of your surroundings but most importantly

it's a spiritual transformation. A spiritual transformation is

seeing my situation and circumstances as God sees them.

When I spiritually re-decorate my waiting room, I adorn my

room with confessions of God's word. The air is filled with

the sounds of praise and worship music. While waiting, I

am setting the atmosphere for God to do WHATEVER He

wants to do. I am no longer focusing on my problems but

on my God who is bigger and greater than any problem.

Instead of crying tears of sorrow, I am praying in the Spirit and crying out for more of Him. My waiting room is no longer a dull, depressing, sad place.

Instead of complaining about the 30 year wait, I now say "God, I'm willing to wait on You forever."

No one can do this but YOU, make a decision that you will seek God for the purpose of your wait. Talk to God every day, read His word and make your waiting room beautiful. Remember, due season always comes and WHAT IF YOURS IS TOMORROW? Or next month?

EXPECT IT, for it will surely come!

Enjoy, your Waiting Room!

Here are a few scriptures for meditation.

Don't copy the behavior and customs of this world, but let God transform you into a new person by changing the way you think. (Romans 12:2, NLT)

Thank You for making me so wonderfully complex! Your workmanship is marvelous-how well I know it. (Psalm 139:14, NLT)

Therefore, if anyone is in Christ, he is a new creation; old things have passed away, and look, new things have come. (II Corinthians 5:17, HCSB)

Strength and dignity are her clothing and her position is strong and secure; she rejoices over the future (the latter day or time to come, knowing that she and her family are in readiness for it)! (Proverbs 31:25, AMP)

But those who wait for the Lord (who expect, look for, and hope in Him) shall change and renew their strength and power; they shall lift their wings and mount up (close to God) as eagles (mount up to the sun); they shall run and not be weary, they shall walk and not faint or become tired. (Isaiah 40:31, AMP)

But as it is written, Eye hath not seen, nor ear heard, neither have entered into the heart of man, the things which God hath prepared for them that love him. (I Corinthians 2:9, KJV)

Chapter 7

Eat My Word

Very early one Saturday morning I was praying and worshipping God. This was during a time where I had been sick for almost 2 weeks with Bronchitis and an upper respiratory infection. I could hardly talk as I prayed and cried out to God. I sat on my sofa and asked God to speak to me. He immediately said okay, turn off the music so that there are no distractions and you can clearly hear Me. So I turned off my worship music and sat in the silence. Silence can be a beautiful thing but silence can also expose some things. God began to tell me that there's nothing wrong with your worship music but there's a time when you need to be silent in My presence to hear. Can you clearly hear AND talk at the same time? Can you sing praise and worship to Me and clearly hear what I'm trying to say to you at the same time? No, you cannot. So I began to tell God that I needed Him and how much I love Him. I asked

Him to heal my body and began thanking Him. After a few seconds God began to clearly speak to me! God said, *"You're crying out for the new but you still haven't completed the old stuff I told you to do".* He said, *"I know that you love Me. I know your heart towards Me. That's why I love you so much. Don't you know that I think about you every day? You are always on My mind. I know about your desires for singing and acting and I know it hurts when you see others around you that are acting in plays and movies. It hurts when others are recording their CD's but nothing has happened for you. Continue to trust Me! I remember the prayer that you prayed that you wrote down to Me! I want to do this new stuff but you have to complete the old stuff that I've told you to do".* God then immediately brought this book back to my mind *(I began writing this book in May 2012)* and told me to write every day. He also told me, *"You're not getting in my Word and reading every day as you should. If you will "eat My word" every day, revelation will begin to flow in your life. You will get the answers on how to help and minister to your children. Solutions to things in your marriage will be found in My word. You won't be going through what you're going through if you just "EAT MY WORD".* He said, *"Continue to trust Me but I also need you to do what you already know you should do. Eat My Word!"*

Those three little words stuck out to me. So God just gave me a hint on how I can get to my BREAKTHROUGH! God just gave "me" a pass code or the key to unlocking my waiting room door!

Hot dog now!! I am on to something!! You mean to tell me that I have sort of prolonged my waiting room stay because of disobedience and laziness?

Yes, I've heard preachers say that everything we need for life can be found in God's word. I believe that and have been a daily bible reader. My Bible app sends me the scripture of the day, I read it and sometimes read the entire chapter (sound familiar?) and then I close my Kindle. I have done my Bible reading for the day and feel good about it. This is the analogy that God showed me.

In the northern states during the winter months, drivers have to spend several minutes and even hours shoveling snow from their porches, driveways and even their cars that are parked outside. This is done just so they can leave their homes and even drive to school or work. They put in lots of hard work scraping and shoveling that snow. God told me, *when you read your scripture of the day it's the same as taking your shovel outside in the snow and scooping up one heaping pile, tossing it to the side, smiling at your accomplishment and going back into the house.* God said, after reading that one scripture, you're still COLD, you're frozen. That one scripture is not enough for you to leave the house and have a victorious day, especially if you just casually read it and don't meditate on it. There's still snow and ice all over you. Just the same as the person who shovels one scoop of snow and think they're going to get their car safely out of the garage without incident. It's not happening! You gotta put in more work! More preparation must be done. If you sat down to eat dinner at your favorite restaurant, would you only eat a spoonful and tell the waiter you're done? No way! You have a juicy, tender steak cooked just the way you ordered it. You have a steaming, loaded baked potato, fresh seasoned steamed vegetables and their signature peach cobbler dessert. There is no way you can eat one or two bites and say you are full or say you have eaten your dinner.

So when God says, "Eat My Word" He expects us to look at it with excitement, anticipation, and expectation that have your taste buds flowing. When we "Eat God's Word" our mindset should be, "I'm going to eat as much of this as I can until I get full". Think about Thanksgiving dinner. Many of us eat so much that we feel as if we're about to burst. We get so full on all that good food. God wants us to be the same way about His word in our waiting rooms. He wants us so full of His word that we burst out with it! When you're full of His word, it changes and transforms you. Then it begins to change and transform everything and everyone around you.

Let me warn you, when you begin to daily eat God's word you may lose a few extra pounds here and there because His word brings life and health to our flesh. If you're physically sick, begin to expect to be healed and to live! His word gives you life, the abundant life! So "EAT MY WORD"!

Here are a few scriptures for meditation.

O taste and see that the Lord (our God) is good! Blessed (happy, fortunate, to be envied) is the man who trusts and takes refuge in Him. (Psalm 34:8, AMPC)

Study and be eager and do your utmost to present yourself to God approved (tested by trial), a workman who has no cause to be ashamed, correctly analyzing, and accurately dividing (rightly handling and skillfully teaching) the Word of Truth. (II Tim. 2:15, AMPC)

Think over these things I am saying (understand them and grasp their application), for the Lord will grant you full insight and understanding in everything. (II Tim. 2:7, AMPC)

Every scripture is God-breathed (given by His inspiration) and profitable for instruction, for reproof and conviction of sin, for correction of error and discipline in obedience, (and) for training in righteousness (in holy living, in conformity to God's will in thought, purpose, and action). (II Tim. 3:16, AMPC)

For the Word that God speaks is alive and full of power (making it active, operative, energizing, and effective); it is sharper than any two-edged sword, penetrating to the dividing line of the breath of life (soul) and (the immortal) spirit, and of joints and marrow (of the deepest parts of our nature), exposing and sifting and analyzing and judging the very thoughts and purposes of the heart. (Hebrews 4:12, AMPC)

Chapter 8

How Bad Do You Want It?

Early one Sunday morning I got up to pray and I was feeling bad in my body. My back was hurting and I was feeling sluggish, old and tired. I sat down in my living room and began to pray. But before I could get a word out God asked me, *"How bad do you want it?"* My initial response was, 'How bad do I want what?' God said,

"Anything and everything you're asking me for, desiring and hoping for. What are you REALLY willing to do to get it? What will you sacrifice? What will you give up and let go of? How bad do you want this thing to MANIFEST in your life? I know all of the excuses, but how BAD do you want it? Are you willing to become radical? Are you ready to STOP making excuses for yourself and why you can't do this or that? Are you ready to just go ALL-IN? Are you ready to experience My glory and feel My presence so strong that you can't speak? I mean so strong that all you

can do is weep and worship Me! Are you truly ready to say

a thing then INSTANTLY see the manifestation? Will you let

go of all that is hindering you and just TRUST ME? I will

NOT allow you to fall. I will NOT leave you alone.

I have everything under My control.

I know what I am doing!

I have done this before.

My end result is guaranteed victory!

I cannot fail. I absolutely cannot lose.

My Word cannot and will not return to Me void, but it shall

and will accomplish EVERYTHING that I purpose it to

accomplish and it will be fruitful!

My Word will deliver!

My Word will prosper and produce in your life!

Don't you know that you're not subject to situations,

problems and sickness? They are subject to you because I

have given YOU the authority that you need to bind and

loose." Glory to God!!!

Matthew18:19 (AMP) says, I will give you the keys of the kingdom of Heaven; and whatever you bind (declare to be improper and unlawful) on earth must be what is ALREADY bound in heaven; and whatever you loose (declare lawful) on earth must be what is ALREADY loosed in heaven.

What are these keys that the Father has given us? I bet you're asking for a set of them! Lol! What if I told you that you ALREADY POSSESS THEM? Yes, this is so exciting! We can bind a thing and loose a thing through our declarations, the words of our mouths. We can bind sickness and loose divine healing when we speak and confess God's word on sickness and healing! We must be strategic with our declarations and prayers! What do you mean by strategic? Well I'm glad you asked. When you're being strategic you have developed a strategy to get what you want. Here's the definition of strategy, and I'll share a few versions.

Strategy- a method or plan chosen to bring about a desired future, such as achievement of a goal or solution to a problem. (businessdictionary.com)

The Merriam-Webster dictionary defines it as: a careful plan or method for achieving a particular goal usually over a long period of time.

Before our awesome military forces are deployed overseas to go to war, a strategy for victory was devised.

Professional football teams have to study and learn plays, they spend hours watching videos. The teams invest in several different coaches for the different positions. (Now I'm no football expert, lol.) The coach develops a strategy. There's the offensive strategy, defensive strategy, special teams strategy, you get the picture. The defensive strategy is to prevent the opposing offense from gaining yards and scoring points. Football teams just don't win because they have nice uniforms or because they have a handsome quarterback. They have developed plays and have a strategy to obtain the win. In like manner, we as believers must develop a strategy for our lives. We must prevent our opponent, Satan, from gaining yards and scoring points in our lives! Everything we do and say must be on purpose and intentional! Develop a strategy for your wait. Develop a strategy for your prayers. Pray strategically! Find scriptures in God's word to back up what you need. Instead of crying and praying, *"Oh Lord, please heal me, Lord I'm sooo tired of hurting. Oh God, please bless me, I'm poor and the devil is on me";* pray God's word!

If you're sick, pray this: *"Father God, I come before You decreeing and declaring Your word over my body. Isaiah 53:5 says that Jesus was wounded for my transgressions and bruised for my guilt and iniquities; the chastisement needful to obtain peace and healing for me was upon Jesus and with the stripes that wounded Jesus, I decree that I AM HEALED AND MADE WHOLE!"*

Declare out of your mouth, *"Jesus has already paid the penalty for my sins. Jesus bore sickness in His body so I wouldn't have to. It is God's desire that I prosper and be in good health."*

"God You said if I bring the tithes into the storehouse so that there are resources in Your house, You would open the windows of heaven and pour me out a blessing that I wouldn't have room enough to contain. So because I am a faithful tither and giver I will not be in lack for You shall supply all my needs. I am blessed to be a blessing. My cup runs over with blessings!

I give and it is given unto me, good measure, pressed down, shaken together and running over! Each day You will give me my daily bread!"

That is what I call strategically praying and I have quoted God's word back to Him as the title deed for what I'm claiming! Glory Hallelujah!!!

"Father God, Your word declares that NO WEAPON that is formed against me shall prosper (Isaiah 54:17). The weapon of sickness (or whatever is attacking you) has formed in my body but I decree and declare by the authority of Your Word that it will NOT prosper against me. I shall live and not die!"

Now what you must do is get you a notebook to write down all the scriptures pertaining to your situation. Do it NOW, by faith! Or I should say scriptures that confirm your "legal right" to having what you are confessing and praying. This is not only about sickness. Strategic prayers will work in ANY area of your life. If you are being attacked in your finances, dealing with disrespectful children, having marital problems or if you're being attacked on your job or being treated unfairly by those in authority over you; strategic prayers must be prayed. Now please make sure your life lines up with your prayers and confessions. You can't pray or confess God's word regarding your job then go to work and curse out your co-worker or join in workplace gossip or mischief. James 1:8 says that by doing such things you are double-minded. What does it mean to be double-minded? Glad you asked.

You have two minds! You are unstable, you waver back and forth!

You confess then you cuss!

You cuss then you confess!

Your loyalty is divided.

One minute you're on God's side and the next minute you're with the world. Now how can you honestly expect to receive ANYTHING from God?

Let's be real about this.

The Message Bible says, you're "keeping all your options open". There should only be ONE option and that's God!

Conclusion

It is my prayer that this book has truly ministered to your spirit and encouraged you in your wait. Allow the Lord to develop, cleanse and prune you in your Waiting Room. Get Ready! Be prepared and ready!

Your number is about to be called and you'll soon be leaving the waiting room. He just called number 298 in the Spirit and you have number 299 (you just don't know it)!! Only you and God know what you need to be doing to PREPARE for what God has for you. Start training and preparing yourself today physically and spiritually. When God completes you and finally calls your waiting room number you'll understand the why's and how's. You'll be a renewed person having a new mindset and a new zeal for God.

I promise, what you shall gain will be well worth the wait! Wait I say on the Lord!

For more information or for bookings please contact

Shondra Echols at shondra56@gmail.com.

Thank you for purchasing this book and may the blessings of our

faithful God be upon you and yours!

Shondra

The following is a prophetic word that God spoke to me on April 25, 2012. I wrote it down exactly as God gave it to me. I hope it blesses and encourages you as much as it has restored, encouraged and strengthened me!!! We are now in the year 2016 and I think it has taken me so long to complete this short book and many other things that God has given me because of offense. My feelings would get hurt over the least little thing and there were times that I had a right to be mad and offended but it still didn't make it right!

Make sure you don't wallow in offense or self pity. Recognize it, release it and forgive every offender. Your skin must be thick for the places you have to go and the things God has for you to do!

Tough Skin
(Prophetic word God spoke to me on 4/25/2012)

Thus says the Lord your God.

I need for you to pray daily, seek My face the way only you know how.

Do not run from Me during times of adversity. These are the times that I am trying to draw you closer to Me. I have not abandoned you, says the Lord. I have not abandoned you!

I know that you are tired, you feel alone and helpless, loveless and forgotten. But I will never abandon you. It may feel like I have forgotten you, but I could never forget you. Do you really know just how precious you are to Me? Do you?

I hear you!

I have heard you!

Shondra, My time is not your time.

My ways are higher than your ways.

What I have begun, I shall finish. Continue to trust Me!

Trust me!

Trust me!

Come to me!

Run to me!

I woke you up early this morning intentionally to tell you this.

Why have you been avoiding Me?

Why have you been running from Me?

Has My word changed? NO!

Can I still do what I said I would do? Yes, most definitely!

I know that you have been waiting for a very long time for your music career to do something. I also know that you have inwardly given up hope. I came to tell you that Tough Skin wins!

Tough Skin Wins! Tough Skin Wins!

You have been abused and beaten by life. You have the scars, bruises, scratches, dark spots and wounds to prove it on your very skin. But as you look at them they can only remind you of how tough your skin is and how you survived every storm that came your way.

Tough Skin Wins!

Shon, I know you are tired. I was tired and frustrated when I had to endure the cross, knowing I had done no wrong. I have also had people who told Me that they loved Me to turn their backs on Me and betray Me. Just like you I know how that feels! I know how it feels to have your character assaulted and to have people lying on you. Your Father knows how you feel!

But this is the key to your breakthrough today!

Just like Jesus got on the cross, he didn't feel like doing it, because it was extremely painful. Jesus did not operate according to His FEELINGS. He operated according to My Word!

Today I say to you, do not live according to your FEELINGS!

No, you will not feel like praying everyday but you need to pray EVERY day!

No, you will not feel like loving your enemies and even praying for them but you need to because they need you to and My Word tells you to.

Shon, the choice is yours.

What are you going to do?

Will you rise up, pursue and conquer? Or will you continue to wallow in self-pity?

Is there an expiration date on trusting Me? No, I've never seen one.

I have already opened doors for you that you cannot see RIGHT NOW.

You have to TRUST ME!

I'm not letting you go! I refuse to let the enemy have you!

I love you too much to let you go! I know EVERYTHING and I STILL love you!

Yes I even remember that, but after you repented I placed it in the sea of forgetfulness, it's no longer on your record!

Stop chasing the studio and chase Me! Stop chasing a recording deal and chase Me!

I AM your provision. I AM whatever you need and can satisfy you greater than anyone or anything else.

I AM all that you need!

Remember when I said tough skin wins? I was talking about you. You are destined to win! I had to allow certain things to happen to you to further toughen your skin and your ministry.

The greater the pain, the greater the gain!

Endure it!

Bear it!

Hold up under the pressure!

Tough Skin wins!

I am cheering for you! And don't you ever forget that!

(I am saying, "You can do it! Go girl!

Come on! Yes! Yes! Look at her go! Father, help her!")

I have always loved you and have wanted My best for you.

Remember that in the end, TOUGH SKIN WINS!